Children *of the* Earth *and* Sky

Children *of the* Earth *and* Sky

Five stories about Native American children
written by Stephen Krensky
illustrated by James Watling

SCHOLASTIC INC.

New York   Toronto   London   Auckland   Sydney

For Joan
—S.K.

To Liza Dee
—J.W.

ISBN 0-590-42853-5

Text copyright © 1991 by Stephen Krensky.
Illustrations copyright © 1991 by James Watling.
All rights reserved. Published by Scholastic Inc.

12 11 10 9 8   3 4 5 6/9

Printed in the U.S.A.   09

First Scholastic printing, November 1991

Introduction

For many thousands of years the only people in North America were Native Americans. These were people whose ancestors had once walked across a land bridge from Siberia to Alaska. They lived here long before anyone arrived from Europe.

Native Americans did not call themselves *Indians*. That was only a name the explorer Christopher Columbus gave them in 1492 because he mistakenly thought he was near India. Actually, Native Americans didn't have any one name because they weren't just one group of people. There were many groups or tribes scattered across the continent.

These tribes lived everywhere — in the forests, the deserts, on the plains, and by the sea. Some were always on the move, others settled in one place. They hunted, fished, or gardened for food. They built homes out of wood, stone, buffalo skins, or adobe mud. It all depended on where they lived.

Although the tribes had many differences between them, their children did share some things in common. They all started helping out their families at a very young age. Their days were a mixture of working and learning and playing.

The children in this book are imaginary, but their world was very real. The tribes included here, the Hopis, Comanches, Mohicans, Navajos, and Mandan, are real, too. The following stories display some of the range and variety of the Native American experience. They are set in a time almost two hundred years ago, when these and other tribes still had much of North America to themselves.

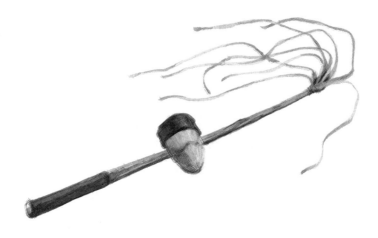

A Hopi Potter

It was a hot day for digging clay. Bright Moon shielded her eyes from the sun as she walked toward the cliffs. The crops growing in the nearby fields looked brittle. They needed rain.

Almost every day was hot in late summer on the mesa. But this summer there had been almost no rain at all. Bright Moon thought it was the driest summer she could remember. And she was nine summers old.

The clay was easy to reach. Bright Moon scooped it out easily from between layers of ancient stone. There were other children gathering clay, too, but Bright Moon kept to herself. Her mother and grandmother were waiting.

It was too bad they could not eat clay. Bright Moon knew that the tribe's supply of corn was running low. Tonight there would be a ceremony for everyone in the village. They would ask the *kachinas,* the Hopi gods, to send rain.

When Bright Moon had collected enough clay, she returned to her home in the pueblo. About two hundred people lived there. The buildings were made from flat slabs of sandstone covered with a mixture of clay, sand, and water. The walls were seven feet high and as thick as her arm was long. They had stood for hundreds of years.

Bright Moon climbed a ladder up to the second floor.

Her grandmother was sitting at the firepit. She was making the batter for *piki*, a very thin, cornmeal bread.

Her mother was sitting by the grinding bin. She helped Bright Moon mix the new clay with sand and crumbled rock. They worked hard, kneading it together with their fingers.

Then Bright Moon started to make her pot. First she patted the paste into a round, flat shape for the base of the bowl. Then she took more of the clay and rolled it between her hands. This was her favorite part. She liked how the soft clay felt, and the way it rolled out longer and thinner as she rubbed her hands together.

When Bright Moon had rolled enough clay, she began coiling it around the base. Higher and higher the clay

looped around. When the pot was the right size, she would smooth the edges with a piece of dried gourd.

Grandmother started to fry the *piki*. She spread the batter thinly over the hot stone griddle. Her fingers moved quickly, dancing over the stone to keep from being burned.

The batter fried quickly. Bright Moon smiled, knowing how her brothers loved the smell of it. But there would be no *piki* for them today. They were out hunting jackrabbits with their father.

While the clay dried, Bright Moon ate with her mother and grandmother. She licked her lips as she bit into the delicious *piki*. Her grandmother made it better than anyone else. She was a clever cook. She knew more ways to cook corn than Bright Moon could remember.

After a time, Bright Moon and her mother returned to the drying pot. They wiped a mixture of fine clay and water on it to fill in the creases between the coils. As the mixture hardened, Bright Moon rubbed the pot with a small stone that fitted comfortably in her hand. It was as smooth as glass, but hard enough to wear down the rough surface.

She rubbed and rubbed until her fingers were sore. Then she showed the pot to her mother, who checked it for bumps and sharp spots.

That finished the pot-making for now. The clay needed to dry some more. Tomorrow Bright Moon would paint it with a black-and-yellow bird pattern. After the paint dried, she would bake the pot to harden the clay.

Bright Moon looked out the window. She saw no sign of her brothers or her father, but she knew they would be

home soon. In tonight's ceremony some of the men, dressed as *kachinas,* would dance. Her father was one of the best dancers in the pueblo. If he and the other men performed well, the spirits of the real *kachinas* would come and possess them. Then the rain would fall.

Bright Moon sighed. The sun still looked very hot. She hoped the *kachinas* would be pleased.

A Comanche Rider

The night was clear, thought Running Wolf, as he stood guarding the horses. The moon was full and rising. The sky was a giant, dark bowl filled with tiny lights. These were travelers, Running Wolf had been told, who began their nightly journeys when the sun had gone.

His horse whinnied softly. The boy patted his horse's flank. They had been together for three summers, ever since Running Wolf was big enough to straddle him. They knew each other well.

Horses were very important to the Comanches. Men rode them into battle and while hunting buffalo. The whole tribe used them to carry *tipis* and other belongings from one campsite to the next.

Running Wolf rubbed his sore shoulder. He had fallen while learning to guide his horse with only his knees. All the boys were taught to ride this way, though they fell many times in the learning. But falls did not matter. Once Running Wolf learned this skill, his hands would be free to hold a bow or a shield.

Running Wolf shifted his weight from one foot to the other. When the moon was overhead, his friend Yellow Star would take his place. Until then, he needed to stay alert. After three more years of training he would be expected to stay awake all night.

Another guard was just barely visible on the far side of the herd. Running Wolf did not call out to him. Four boys in all were watching the herd. They were not playing a game. Some tribes stole horses from other tribes. Horses were very valuable. Sometimes hunters spent several days and nights running down wild horses. Running Wolf and Yellow Star looked forward to that time, when they, too, would catch wild horses and hunt buffalo together.

Suddenly, a twig cracked. Running Wolf pulled out his knife, made from a buffalo's rib. An owl hooted nearby.

Running Wolf smiled and put away his knife. He knew that owl. It was Thundercloud. His friend tried hard, but he really didn't sound much like an owl at all.

Thundercloud had known the boys would be hungry. The night before, when he had been on guard, no one had

remembered to feed him. Tonight he had brought his friends chunks of meat that had been broiled over the fire. He gave the meat to Running Wolf and moved on to find the other guards.

Running Wolf ate quickly. He stayed alert to the landscape. It would not be good to have horses stolen while he was busy filling his stomach. In the nearby camp, the last of the fires were dying, the burning buffalo chips turning to ashes. Running Wolf did not think of the warm *tipi,* of sleeping under a blanket. The cold did not matter. Neither did being alone.

He stood tall in the darkness and watched the night pass.

A Mohican Hunter

At the first sign of day, Red Leaf awoke in his family's dome-shaped *wigwam*. Its birchbark shell had kept out the snow during the night, but the wind had sometimes crept in. Red Leaf felt warm, though, under several thick furs.

Still, he was eager to get up and explore. In the past few days his tribe had crossed many hills and valleys. The hunting was not rich enough for the tribe to stay in any one place all winter. Everything Red Leaf's family owned — their clothes, their tools, even their home — he and his mother and father carried with them.

Red Leaf wrinkled his nose. He could smell the root soup his mother was making outside. The hunting had been bad lately, and he had eaten a lot of root soup. Still, it was better than nothing.

After he ate, Red Leaf set off into the forest. The new snow covered the ground in a hard white shell. He carried his bow and arrows and a crooked knife made from a beaver tooth. He also carried some meat scraps to use as bait for a trap.

Red Leaf had planned to go hunting with his friend Small Fox. But Small Fox had stayed behind to help repair his family's *wigwam*. An icy branch had fallen on it during the night.

As Red Leaf walked through the forest, he felt slow and awkward. His winter buckskin was bulky. It was much easier to hunt in the summer when he didn't have to wear it.

But winter could be fun, too. When there was time, he played snowsnake with his friends. They took turns throwing a snakelike spear along a frozen track. Whoever threw the spear the farthest would win. Sometimes Red Leaf threw the spear so hard he lost his balance and fell down.

Red Leaf stopped suddenly. There were many animal tracks in the snow. Perhaps this path led to water. It would be a good place to build a deadfall.

Red Leaf looked around. He pulled half of a rotted log out onto the path. It was almost as big as he was. He sharpened the ends of two forked branches with his knife and pushed them into the ground. Then he propped the log up on top of them. Next he put some bait under the log. When an animal came forward to eat, the animal would

knock out the branches and the log would crash down on it. Red Leaf would come back for the animal later.

For now, Red Leaf continued to explore. When he came to the next clearing, he stopped short. There across the meadow was a deer.

Red Leaf pulled out an arrow and fingered the three little feathers spaced around its shaft. He would have to move closer, closer than a stone's throw, to hit the deer with an arrow. His bow wasn't strong enough for a longer shot.

As he took a step forward, the snow crunched under his foot.

The deer looked up, stared at him for an instant, and bounded away.

Small Fox came running up behind him. He had seen the whole thing. No one could have caught that deer, he said. It was smarter than a raccoon and as fast as the wind. He and Red Leaf would catch another deer.

But they saw no more deer that morning. At midday they started back to camp. It was still too soon to find anything in the deadfall. They would check it again the next day. Both boys sighed at the thought of nothing but nuts and more root soup for supper.

But when they returned to camp, they learned the good news. Three older hunters had killed two deer. There would be plenty of food after all.

And maybe some time to play snowsnake.

A Navajo Weaver

Standing in the middle of a wide plain, Little Crow looked out at fingers of striped rock reaching toward the sky. The morning was bright and clear. She felt comfortable in her shirt, skirt, and moccasins all made of buckskin. A slight breeze brushed her hair, which was parted in the middle and drawn into a knot behind her neck.

Little Crow could see her brother standing in the distance. He was helping their father guard the family's flock of sheep. The wool they got from the sheep was very important. It was used to make clothing and blankets. The whole family helped with the shearing, but only the women did the weaving.

Her mother was setting up the loom in the *ramada*. This was an open brush-covered frame with four poles at the corners. The loom was made of two upright poles and two crossbars, which supported the warp frame.

Little Crow was glad they did not have to weave inside their *hogan*. The *hogan* was a warm house to sleep in at night, but it was dark and stuffy. Its log walls and roof were caked with mud and did not let much air through. And there were no openings besides the doorway and the smoke hole in the roof.

The sun's warmth felt good on Little Crow's face. She was glad spring had come. Only a month before, her family had still been living at their winter *hogan*. Her people did not live in one village all year round. Families moved to different *hogans* with the seasons, following their grazing sheep.

Her mother called out to her. It was time to get the wool.

Little Crow went back inside the dark *hogan*. She walked softly on the swept dirt floor, ducking under some trinkets hanging from the beams. The balls of wool were in a basket next to a pile of bedding rolled up against the wall.

Little Crow fingered the brown and white wool. She had cleaned this wool herself, straightening the tangled strands and unraveling the many knots. She had helped to spin it, too.

When she returned outside, her mother was ready to begin. She used a simple spindle — a smooth, slender, hardwood stick about two feet long. She pushed it through

a thin, wooden disc as wide as her hand. Her mother began at the bottom. Her fingers were a blur as she moved the batten. The comb darted in and out of the yarn.

Little Crow sighed. She wondered if she would ever be so skilled.

Her mother paused and motioned her forward. It was her turn. Little Crow's fingers were clumsy at first. She stopped and started a lot. The wool got bunched and knotted. It was hard to keep track of so many things at once.

Patiently her mother straightened and smoothed the wool. She reminded Little Crow that she, too, had once stumbled with her fingers. What she did now her grandmother had also done, and her grandmother before that.

The hours passed quickly as mother and daughter worked together. They took a short break for a midday meal of broiled rabbit left over from the night before. Little Crow was too excited to eat very much.

When her brother and father returned home that evening, Little Crow showed them her work. There was barely a finger width to look at, but she described in great detail the striped pattern she had planned. It was not much of a blanket yet, but the work was hers. She was very proud.

Mandan Gardeners

Spotted Deer and her younger brother, Gray Hawk, started off together for their garden near the river. The sun was shining, but the air was chilly. Spring came late to the Northern Plains.

It had been a very busy morning. When a girl had lived eight winters, there were many things to do. Spotted Deer had already fetched wood and water. She had helped her mother prepare the morning meal. While her mother began weaving a basket, Spotted Deer took care of her baby sister. When it was time to leave for the garden, her mother's hands were still busy, so Spotted Deer put the baby in her cradleboard and hung it on a nearby tree.

Spotted Deer looked forward to the gardening. She liked helping things grow. Gray Hawk was excited, too. He was bringing along his bow and arrows. He had been practicing with them for a long time. He had never hit anything with an arrow, but the birds did not know that. Gray Hawk would guard the seeds after his sister planted them. The birds would not get to eat them.

Spotted Deer and Gray Hawk found the garden just as they had left it. The patch of land was already dug up into rows. On other days Gray Hawk had raked the ground with a deer antler for many hours. Spotted Deer had dug furrows, using a hoe made from a long stick and the shoulder bone of a buffalo. Both of them had mixed food scraps into the soil to make it richer.

Now it was time to plant the corn and squash and beans. Spotted Deer knelt down with her seeds. She carefully made a hole with a pointed stick, raking it back and forth. She then dropped in the seed and covered it up.

A crow squawked from a nearby tree. Gray Hawk raised his bow and stared at the bird. The crow came no closer.

When Spotted Deer finished the sixth row, the sun was high overhead. Both she and Gray Hawk were hungry. They sat down on a shaded rock to eat *pemmican*. It was made from chokecherries pounded together with meat and fat. They ate *pemmican* often. It didn't spoil, and it didn't have to be cooked.

From where they sat, the children had a good view of

their village. It was built on a bluff above the river. The spot had been carefully chosen. Lookouts would be able to give the villagers plenty of warning about the approach of friends or enemies.

The children could also see the gardens of many other families. Their tribe had cultivated all the rich land near the river. Many tribes who lived on the Plains had to move often, following the herds of buffalo or other sources of food. But the Mandan, because they grew so much of what they ate, did not need to hunt so widely. This had allowed them to settle in one place and build larger, more comfortable homes. Their round lodges were forty to sixty feet wide and fifteen feet high. Each one was built sturdily of forked poles and crossbeams covered with grassy mattings and mud.

Gray Hawk jumped to his feet as three more crows settled on a nearby branch. He raised his bow and shouted at them. The crows fluttered their wings and cawed back.

Spotted Deer smiled. Then she returned to her work. She had many more seeds to plant before sunset, but she was not worried. The garden would be safe with a guard as fierce as Gray Hawk.

Afterword

For the Native American children of long ago, skills such as hunting or weaving were not hobbies or games. They were important parts of everyday life. The different tribespeople had to make just about everything they used, and so they took very little for granted.

Native Americans of long ago paid close attention to the world around them because they couldn't afford not to. Today our attention is often distracted by other things. But even though the world has changed, there is still much we can learn from the Native American way of life.

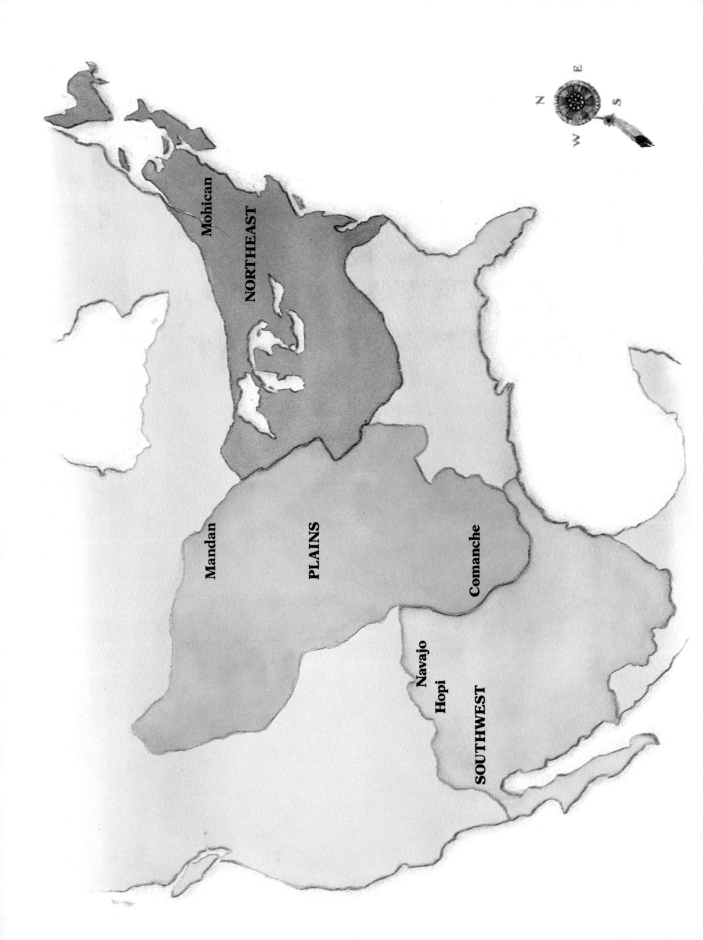

Glossary

Hopi *pueblo*

The **Hopis** were a peaceful people of the Southwest, some of whose *pueblos* were a thousand years old. They long maintained their independence from other tribes and from European contact.

Comanche *tipi*

The **Comanches** were one of the fiercest tribes of the Plains. The most skilled of horsemen, they fought with almost all other tribes they met.

Mohican *wigwam*

The **Mohicans** were part of the Algonquin family, whose tribes were spread over the Northeast. Their home in the forests of the Adirondacks changed with the seasons.

Navajo *hogan*

The **Navajos** were the largest Native American tribe. After moving to the Southwest in the 1700s, they adopted many art forms from the Hopis.

Mandan lodge

The **Mandan** were among the few Plains tribes to live in one place. Instead of roaming after the buffalo herds on horseback, they based their lives on agriculture.